First published 1982
Second impression 1983
The Hamlyn Publishing Group Limited
London · New York · Sydney · Toronto
Astronaut House, Feltham, Middlesex, England

ISBN 0 600 36670 7

These stories first appeared in *The Enid Blyton Pennant Series* published in 1950 by Macmillan & Co. Limited.

Printed in Italy

Mike's monkey

and other stories

Enid Blyton

Illustrated by Val Biro

Hamlyn

London · New York · Sydney · Toronto

Contents

Mike's monkey

When Mike's birthday came his uncle Ned gave him a queer present. It was a little brown monkey!

'Here you are!' said Uncle Ned, and he put the monkey into Mike's arms. 'Here's a little monkey for you. He's quite young, so you can teach him anything. He'll copy all you do and give you a lot of fun.'

'Well,' said Mother, 'I hope he treats his monkey better than he treats his toys. He is always breaking those. And he hardly has a nice book left, he tears the pages so.'

It was quite true. Mike did spoil his things dreadfully. He broke so many, he left his toys out in the rain, he spoilt his books, and broke all his chalks.

'You destroy all your nice things,' his mother said to him. 'You really must get out of the habit. Look at that nice teddy bear you had—you've pulled out all his whiskers and cut off his ears. That's very naughty of you.'

Anyway, Mike couldn't do that kind of thing to a live monkey. And he didn't want to, for he loved the little thing. It slept in Mike's wheelbarrow, covered by a little rug. It ate fruit, and loved a bit of cucumber. It had the funniest ways, and Mike loved it very much.

It went with him everywhere, sitting on his shoulder. It copied everything he did. It even learnt to hold a cup by the handle and drink from it.

It copied Mike when he cleaned his teeth. It copied him when he brushed his hair—except that the monkey brushed its nose instead of its hair!

One day Mike was in the nursery, playing with his toys. He was in one of his naughty moods. He broke his little sailor doll. He broke his engine. He tore a whole page out of a book. He took a pencil and scribbled all over the door of the toy cupboard.

The monkey watched him. It liked to do everything that Mike did. It took a flower vase off the mantelpiece and threw it on the floor, where it broke.

Then it threw down the clock. Mike was full of horror. Whatever would Mother say! The monkey took some books from the bookcases and began to tear pages out of them, just as it had seen Mike do. When Mike tried to stop it, it leapt to the top of the curtain, where Mike couldn't reach it, and went on tearing out pages.

Then it leapt down, took Mike's pencil and began to scribble all over the walls of the room. Mike knew his mother would be very angry indeed.

So she was. When she came in, she glared at Mike and said: 'So you are in one of your naughty moods! Look at my clock, and my vase! Look at those books, all torn! And just see this dreadful scribbling all over the walls!'

'Mother—the monkey did it,' said Mike, afraid that he was going to get a whipping.

'Then if that is so, the monkey will have to go,' said Mother at once. 'I'm not going to have everything destroyed like this. What a naughty little creature!'

'Oh, Mother—it wasn't really the monkey's fault,' said Mike. 'It was mine. I was naughty first. I broke Sailor Doll, and my engine, and I tore a book. And I scribbled over the toy cupboard door.'

'I see,' said Mother. 'Well—I will forgive the monkey this time. As for you, you will go to bed for the rest of the day.'

The next morning was fine, so Mike and the monkey went out of doors. Mike had a horrid way of knocking the heads off the daisies with a stick—he did so like spoiling things, which was a very bad habit. He picked up a stick and began to

swish the heads off all the flowers in the grass.

The monkey thought that was a good idea. It took up a stick too, and went to a bed of flowers. Soon it was knocking all the heads off, and the gardener came rushing up in a rage.

'Look at that! I'll tell your mother! I won't have a monkey like that in the garden if it's going to spoil all my work. I'll tell your mother.'

He did—and Mother said that settled it, the monkey had got to go.

Mike wept and wailed. He loved his monkey. It wouldn't be happy without him. He wanted it so badly. It might die if it hadn't got him to look after it.

'Now look here, Mike,' said his mother, 'it's no good making all this fuss. It's all your own fault and you know it. You have this bad habit of breaking and spoiling things for no reason at all, and the monkey copies you in everything. Whenever you spoil things, as you so often do, the monkey is going to spoil things too, so there will be two stupid people instead of one.'

'I didn't know I was so bad about spoiling things,' wept Mike. 'I just did it without thinking. Now I see my monkey doing it too, I do see how horrid it is. Give the monkey another chance, Mother, please do. I love him so.'

Mother didn't say anything for a minute. Then she spoke more gently. 'I'll give **you** another chance, Mike, and see if you really do want to keep the monkey, and love him as much as you say you do. It rests with you whether you keep him or not. Get out of this silly habit of spoiling things, and the monkey will no longer copy you in that, and he can stay.'

'Oh, I will, I will!' said Mike, drying his eyes.

'But if you break or tear or spoil anything again for no reason at all, and the monkey does the same, he will have to go,' said Mother. 'Now we will see if you love him enough to behave yourself.'

Mike took the tiny monkey into his arms. The little creature nestled there, looking up at him with bright eyes, for it loved Mike.

'I didn't know how silly I was to destroy things till you showed me, Monkey,' said Mike. 'Don't you get into bad habits like I have. Get into good ones! I'll try and get good ones too, and then you can copy them.'

That was a week ago. You will be glad to know that the monkey is still with Mike. I do hope Mike will be able to keep the little thing, don't you?

Eyes and No-Eyes

There were once two brothers, but they were not a bit alike. One was fair and the other was dark. One was fat and the other wasn't. And one used his eyes and noticed everything, and the other didn't.

Tom was the dark, small lively one. Tim was the fair, dull one. Their teacher used to get cross with Tim.

'You never use your eyes or your ears!' he said. 'You never notice anything! Look at Tom now—he always notices everything: the birds, the trees, the weather, people —and he hears what I say to him too, and does what I ask!'

'Well, I get along all right,' said

Tim, in a grumbling tone. 'Tom's so sharp he'll cut himself one day. I can't be bothered to be as smart as he is.'

'I shall call Tom "Eyes", and I shall call you "No-Eyes",' said the teacher. 'Eyes and No-Eyes—that's just what you two brothers are. Now for goodness' sake, Tim, try to be a bit livelier—wake up and use your eyes and ears a bit more.'

Tim grumbled to Tom on the way home. 'What is the use of having eyes that dart around like yours and never miss anything? It's too tiring. What good does it do you or anyone else either?'

'Well, I like noticing everything,' said Tom. 'It's interesting. And who knows, one day it may do somebody else good too, besides making me happy.'

Every day the two boys walked to school, and you would have been surprised to know all that Eyes noticed and No-Eyes missed.

Eyes saw the big black cat washing itself, he saw the starlings trying to sing on the roofs, he saw how green the trees were getting, he felt the stickiness of the chestnut buds, he noticed the smoke that curled up from the little cottage at the level crossing gate, and he listened for the express train that sometimes came rushing by just before they got into school.

No-Eyes saw nothing at all except the pavement below him. He never bothered to look around and see things. It was too much trouble.

Now one day when the two boys went to school, Eyes as usual looked all round him to notice everything. Yes, the black cat was there. It had had fish for breakfast, because there was a fish bone stuck on one of its whiskers.

The chestnut buds were bursting open. Good, that meant that spring was coming, although it was very cold that day. The wind was in the north, as Eyes could see from the weathercock on the roof of the church.

His glance swung down from the weathercock to the little cottage by the level crossing, where the trains rushed by at certain times of the day.

Usually there was a spire of smoke from the chimney of the little cottage. Mrs. Williams lived there all alone. She opened the gates for the trains to go through and shut them again when they had gone, so that people could walk across the line.

But today Eyes noticed that there was no smoke coming from Mrs. Williams's red chimney. He wondered why.

'Look, Tim,' he said, stopping. 'Mrs. Williams hasn't got a fire today. She must be very cold without one.'

'How do you know she hasn't got a fire?' said No-Eyes in surprise.

'Because there isn't smoke from her chimney,' said Eyes. 'It's funny. She feels the cold very much, and always keeps a big fire—and it's a very cold day. Why hasn't she got a fire?'

'Because she's run out of coal,' said No-Eyes, feeling clever.

'You can see her pile of coal in the backyard from here,' said Eyes. 'It isn't that. I think, Tim, I'll just run along and see why Mrs. Wil-

liams hasn't a fire today.'

'You'll be late for school,' said No-Eyes. 'You're silly. Fancy bothering about whether someone has a fire or not, just because you don't see their chimney smoke as usual.'

'All the same, I'm going to see,' said Eyes, and off he went. He came to the little cottage. The milk was outside the door and so was the morning paper. That was queer. Mrs. Williams hadn't taken them in. Why not? The boy knocked on the door, but nobody answered.

He peeped in at the window, and what a shock he got! Poor Mrs. Williams had fallen off her little ladder, when she was putting her curtains right, and had bumped her head so hard that she had fainted. There she lay—no fire lighted—no one to see her—quite alone.

'Goodness!' said Eyes suddenly. 'What about the express train? It's due in a minute—and the gates are still shut!'

As he spoke, he heard the roar of the train as it was coming along. Quick as lightning the boy rushed to open the gates. He pushed hard, and the gates slowly opened for the train to go through. Only just in time too, for the express roared by before Eyes had taken his hands off the second gate.

'Another minute and the train might have been off the lines,' said Eyes, and he found that he was trembling. He put little Mrs. Williams on the sofa and bathed her face with cold water. She opened her eyes.

‘The express,’ she said. ‘The express!’

‘It’s all right. I opened the gates. It’s gone through safely,’ said Tom. ‘I’ll fetch someone to help you.’

He found Mrs. Williams's sister, and she hurried to help. Eyes raced off to school, but he was late. He didn't like to say why, because it seemed like boasting, so he got a scolding.

But his teacher soon knew all about it, for Mrs. Williams told everyone how Tom had come along

and found her, opened the gates, and fetched help.

'He's a good boy, that,' she said. 'I wonder how he guessed I was in need of help. The express might have been badly shaken if he hadn't come.'

'How **did** you know, Eyes?' asked his teacher.

'Well—only because I noticed that no smoke was coming out of Mrs. Williams's chimney,' said Tom. 'That made me wonder a bit, and I went to see why. That's all.'

'Ah—now we see the difference between Eyes and No-Eyes!' said the teacher. 'Tom used his eyes and his brain and saved the express from an accident. Tim saw nothing. You deserve a reward, Tom. Well done.'

Tom got a reward, though he didn't want one. It was a silver watch, given to him by the railway company. He is very proud of it, and it really is a lovely one.

I'd rather be Eyes than No-Eyes, wouldn't you? You never know when you might do something very brave because you used your eyes.

The very old teddy bear

Bruiny, the teddy bear, was very old indeed. He belonged to Billy, and he was older even than Billy, because once upon a time he had belonged to Billy's mother.

Billy's mother had loved him very

much, and she had never wanted to give him away. But when she had a little boy of her own, she brought old Bruiny out of the cupboard and gave him to Billy.

'There you are!' she said. 'You can have old Bruiny, darling. He's so soft and cuddlesome. He's had to be sewn up here—and here—and his ears don't match now—but I expect you will love him because he looks so sweet.'

Billy did love him. He was such a very cuddly bear. You know, some toys are much more cuddly than others, and you feel as if you must snuggle them up in bed. Well, Bruiny was that kind of toy. He was lovely in bed.

Billy loved him very much. He played with Bruiny a lot when he was little. Then he came to the time when he liked engines and cars, and he played with those all day.

New toys came to the nursery. There was a very neat sailor doll. There was a clockwork dog that could run and wag its tail. There were two soldiers, both as smart as could be.

They laughed at old Bruiny. 'Whatever does Billy keep you for?' they said. 'A dirty, smelly old toy like you! You look awful. Your ears don't match—and did you know you have lost an eye?'

'Yes. I know,' said Bruiny. 'It fell down a crack in the floor. I couldn't get it out.'

'You ought to be put in the dust-bin,' said the clockwork dog in disgust. 'I don't like living in the same toy cupboard as you!'

'He won't be kept much longer,' said the sailor doll. 'Billy will throw him away—he's too old even to **give** away now!'

'Don't let's talk to him,' said one of the soldiers. 'Really, he's quite impossible!'

But the bear didn't seem to mind what they said. He smiled a little, and looked at them out of his one brown eye.

'You don't seem to mind the idea of being thrown away!' said the sailor doll, annoyed.

'I shan't be thrown away,' said Bruiny.

'Well, you might be given away, or thrown into the back of the cupboard and never remembered again,' said the clockwork dog.

'I shan't be forgotten, or given away,' said Bruiny. 'I may fall to bits with old age—but I shan't be put into the dustbin—and I dare say I shall still be here when **you** are all broken and gone.'

'What does he mean?' said the sailor doll to the two soldiers. 'He seems very sure about things. How does he know he won't be thrown away?'

'He sits there and smiles, and he doesn't care a bit when we say these things to him,' said one of the soldiers, puzzled.

'Dirty, ragged, smelly, ugly old thing!' said the clockwork dog. 'I'd be afraid of the dustbin every minute of the day, if I was like him!'

Bruiny wasn't unhappy or worried. He just looked rather amused, as if he knew something that the others didn't know. They were so curious about it that at last they asked him.

'Why are you so sure that nothing horrid will happen to you?' said the sailor doll at last. 'Tell us. You look as if you know something that we don't know.'

'I do,' said Bruiny. 'I know the biggest thing in the world, the only

thing that can be trusted, and the most beautiful thing there is. And I know I am safe as long as it lasts.'

'How are you safe? What do you know? What is the biggest thing in the world?' said the other toys in surprise.

'Listen to me and I will tell you,' said the teddy bear, looking at them out of his one brown eye. 'What do you see when you look at me? I know very well! You see a dirty old bear, sewn up here and there because he got torn, with ears that don't match, and with only one eye, and no growl!'

He stopped. The others nodded. That was just what they did see.

'Well, Billy sees all that too, but it doesn't matter to him, because he loves me,' said Bruiny. 'Love is the very biggest thing in the world, you know. I'm safe because Billy loves me. **He** won't put me into the dust-bin, **he** won't give me away. I'm Bruiny, the old bear he loves, the old bear his mother loved too, the old bear that has snuggled up to him hundreds and hundreds of times!'

'Oh,' said the sailor doll. 'He must love you a lot, Bruiny.'

'He does,' said Bruiny. 'Some toys are always loved more than others, you know, just as some people are loved more than others. I'm a lucky bear, because I've been loved a lot. I've loved Billy's mother too, and of course I love Billy. No wonder I'm happy.'

'Yes. No wonder you are happy,' said the clockwork dog. 'I'd like to be loved like that too. You must feel very safe when you are loved. It's a pity there isn't more love in the world, Bruiny. There doesn't seem enough to go round.'

'There is really,' said Bruiny, 'but we don't all do our share, and love one another. I know you hate me, for instance—but I can't help being old and ragged.'

'No—we don't hate you,' said the sailor doll, looking suddenly ashamed. 'We weren't very wise, that's all. We didn't think about this biggest thing in the world. Please be friends, will you?'

'Of course,' said Bruiny, delighted. 'I'll do anything I can for you—I'll tell you stories of the time when Billy's mother was a little girl, if you like. I know such a lot of stories.'

But before he could tell them one, Billy came in. 'Where's old Bruiny?' he said. 'Oh, there you are. Come along, Bruiny, I want to cuddle you tonight, because I feel lonely. Mother's gone away for a bit, you know. We'll snuggle up in bed together, dear old cuddly bear!'

'How Billy loves Bruiny!' said the sailor doll to the others. 'No wonder he feels safe. It must be nice to be loved like that. Let's be friendly and loving to him now—shall we?—because he really is such a nice old bear.'

I expect you wonder what has happened to old Bruiny. Well, he belongs to Billy's little sister now, and **she** takes him to bed every night, and loves him. So he knows quite a lot about the biggest thing in the world, doesn't he—lucky old bear!

The angry pixies

The children loved to go for a picnic in Pixie Wood. It was such a beautiful place. Primroses shone there by the hundred, violets smelt sweetly, and bluebells made a wonderful carpet in May time.

One day, when the primroses were out, Joan, Harry, Peter and Lucy went to the woods to have a picnic. They took with them packets of sandwiches and cakes, a big bar of chocolate, two bottles of lemonade, and some plastic cups to drink

from.

'We shall have a lovely picnic,' said Harry. 'My mother has made egg and cress sandwiches.'

'And mine has made jam ones,' said Joan. 'We can share them all out and have some of each.'

They found a beautiful dell in the woods, and sat down to have their picnic. How good the food tasted. The children sat and looked round them as they ate.

Primroses shone pale and yellow all about them. Anemones nodded in the breeze. Violets nestled close to the primroses, and birds sang all round. The green moss was as soft as smooth velvet.

A robin sat in a bush and looked at them. He was hoping for a crumb. Harry saw him. He picked up a stone and threw it at the robin.

'Don't!' said Joan. 'Poor little thing—you hit it!'

The robin flew away with a cry of

pain. It did not come back again. A tiny rabbit peeped at them from behind a tree. 'Isn't he sweet?' said Lucy. But he didn't peep long because Peter threw a stick at him. He ran into his hole and didn't come back any more.

'I've finished my dinner,' said Harry. 'Let's put these lemonade bottles up on that stone over there, and throw stones at them. We'll see who can break them first.'

So they did. Harry was the best. He broke both bottles, and bits of glass flew all over the primroses and green moss. Peter began to throw bits of moss at the others.

'Don't,' said Lucy. 'Let's play a proper game, Peter. Don't let's throw any more things.

So they played 'He', and in their excitement they trampled on the primroses and violets, and broke down the dancing anemones.

The wind came into the dell and blew the sandwich papers about. But nobody bothered to pick them up. The plastic cups were trodden on and lay in the dell too.

Soon Peter looked at his watch. 'Almost time to go,' he said. 'Shall we dig up a few primrose roots to take home?'

They dug up the best ones and then they went home, thinking what a lovely picnic they had had.

Now, the next day, Harry went into the woods again. He was on his way to see his uncle, who lived on the other side of the woods. He hadn't gone very far before he heard a loud and angry voice.

'I shall tell the policeman! It's a wicked shame! I shall go and tell the policeman now!'

Harry peeped to see who was speaking. He saw a small pixie-man, and he was surprised and pleased, for he had never seen one of the Little Folk before.

'What's the matter?' said Harry. 'Can I help you?'

'What do you think has happened?' said the pixie angrily. 'I had a most beautiful home in these woods, and the prettiest garden you ever saw, with primroses, violets and anemones growing all round. And I had a robin for a friend, and a little rabbit too. I had moss for a carpet, and I kept everything as neat as could be. And now somebody has spoilt it all!'

'What a pity!' said Harry.

'Yes—they've stolen some of my primroses, trampled on all my flowers, and dug up my moss,' said the pixie, angry tears running down his cheeks. 'And do you know, one of them has broken my robin's leg? Think of that!'

'Oh,' said Harry.

'And they frightened away my little rabbit and he won't come and talk to me,' said the pixie; 'but worst of all, they left broken glass all over the place, and when I got back late last night in the dark, I trod on it, cut my shoes to pieces and hurt my foot!'

Harry saw that the pixie's foot was bound up in a white rag. The little man went on, getting more and more upset as he talked.

'They left their rubbish there too —bits of paper and things like that. How dare they? What would they say if anyone did all that in **their** gardens?'

'Perhaps they didn't know it was

your garden,' said Harry, very red in the face.

'Well, even if they didn't, surely they had the sense to know that other people might want to come and enjoy the beauty of the woods!' cried the pixie. 'Why should people spoil beautiful things? They must have very ugly minds if they can't see these woods are lovely. They must be horrid, selfish people, and I am going to the policeman who lives

in the heart of the woods, to tell him to punish them. He's a pixie policeman who knows all kinds of magic. You come and tell him too.'

'I must get home, thank you,' said Harry, and before the pixie could say another word, he ran all the way home. He found Joan, Peter and Lucy, and told them about the angry pixie and all he had said.

'He was quite right,' said Joan, looking ashamed of herself. 'We did spoil that lovely dell—and oh, Harry, that poor, poor little robin! Did you really break its leg?'

Lucy had tears in her eyes. She loved birds. She didn't like to think of the frightened rabbit either. How **could** they have behaved like that?

'We'll go and tell that pixie that we're very sorry and we'll never behave like that again,' said Lucy. So they all went to find him. But he wasn't there. The dell lay silent in the sunshine, spoilt and trampled.

'The pixie must have moved,' said Lucy. 'Let's pick up our rubbish. What a pity we can't say we're sorry and won't ever do such a thing again. I wish we could see the pixie.'

But they never did. Still, they kept their word, and now, when they go for a picnic, they are just like you, and never spoil anything, never throw stones, and always take their rubbish back in a bag. So they should, shouldn't they?

Sally the screamer

When Sally didn't get what she wanted, she screamed. Then, when she screamed, her mother gave her what she wanted, and that was very bad for her, wasn't it?

Her mother should have been

sensible, and said, 'Now, Sally, if you want to scream, you can—but you must scream somewhere that no one can hear you, because it is a very horrid noise. So go upstairs to your room, shut the door and scream by yourself!'

Then Sally would have stopped screaming at once, because it isn't any good screaming when nobody can hear you. You don't get what you are screaming for then.

So, as her mother didn't say that, Sally went on screaming for what she wanted, making such a terrible noise that her mother always gave in. The little girl soon became very bad-tempered, and screamed more and more.

One day when she was screaming because her mother said she couldn't go out when she wanted to, an old woman popped her head in at the window.

'I say!' she said, 'you'll scream the house down.'

Sally stopped screaming for a moment to see the old woman. She

didn't like her. So she opened her mouth and screamed twice as loudly, hoping that her mother would come and send the old woman away.

The old woman stopped up her ears, and looked up at the ceiling, as if she really expected the house to fall down.

'I'm afraid you **will** scream the house down today,' she said. 'I can see a bit of the ceiling coming loose already. Come with me and I'll take you to a house that is already tumbling down. It will be quite a help if you scream **that** down.'

Before Sally could run away the old woman reached a long arm into the room, and jerked her out of the window. Then she ran with her at top speed down the street, into the wood and down a path that Sally had never seen before.

Sally screamed and screamed. She went purple in the face because she was so angry. 'That's right,' said the old woman. 'Go on screaming. Don't stop, Sally. We are nearly there. Scream away as loudly as you can.'

Sally did. She couldn't get away from the queer old woman, who hurried her along through the wood as fast as she could go. They came at last to a tumbledown house, where no one lived.

'Here we are,' said the old woman.

'This house is to be pulled down, and the builders are going to make me a nice new little house. But they have been too busy to pull it down, so if you scream the house down for me, that will be a great help.'

She pushed Sally into the house and shut the door. She called to her through a window: 'Now scream loudly, child! Open your mouth wide, feel as angry as you can, and scream! Go on!'

Sally was so very, very angry that she did scream loudly. You should have heard her. The noise made all the birds around jump in fright, and fly away.

'Good! Good!' said the old woman. 'You've screamed down the wall, look—and there goes a door!'

To Sally's horror, she saw one of the walls falling down—and then a door fell in. Dust flew all over the place. Sally didn't like it at all.

'Let me out, let me out!' she shouted. 'The house is falling down! I shall be hurt.'

'Well, I want you to scream it down for me,' said the old woman. 'No—you are not to come out till you have screamed it all down for me. Then I can have a nice new house built up.'

Sally beat on the front door and screamed with rage. How dare the old woman keep her there when she wanted to get out! She screamed so loudly that the chimneypots fell off with a clatter. Then another wall fell down, and bricks toppled everywhere. Sally screamed again—but this time with fright.

'I'm frightened! Let me out!'

'No, go on screaming with rage a bit longer,' said the old woman. 'There's still a lot of the house to fall down yet.'

Sally opened her mouth to scream with rage—and then she shut it again. She looked round. Why, the roof might easily fall on her! The windows might tumble in on top of her and cut her. Why should she scream the house down for this horrid old woman? She **wouldn't** scream.

'Go on with your bad temper,' said the old woman. 'Scream, my dear, scream, as you always do when you can't get what you want. It isn't often I can get a child to help scream my house down for me, I can tell you.'

Sally was angry, full of bad temper and fright—but she stopped herself from screaming. It was the first time in her life that she had stopped screaming before she had got her own way. She didn't like it. But it was good for her.

'I'm not going to scream any more,' she shouted to the old woman. 'I won't. I shan't scream your house down for you. So you can let me go. I'm not going to scream any more.'

'Are you sure?' said the old woman. Sally nodded, keeping her mouth shut in case a scream suddenly came out by itself. The old woman opened the door and let Sally out.

'Well, if you won't scream my house down for me, I suppose I'll have to let you go home,' she said. 'But I'll soon have you back here, my dear—you'll be screaming with rage again before long, I've no doubt. Then I'll rush you off to my tumbledown house, and you can scream a bit more of it down.'

Sally said nothing—but she made up her mind that never, never would she scream that old woman's house down for her. Never.

'I suppose it means I must never scream again when I'm in a temper or want something,' she thought. 'Still, I won't. I'm not going to have that house tumbling round about my head.'

So she didn't scream any more, and her mother wondered why. Sometimes Sally opened her mouth to scream, but before the scream came out, she always remembered, shut it again, and tried to forget her bad temper.

The old woman's house is still there, waiting for someone to scream it down. If you know anyone who has a bad temper and screams, you might let her know.

Which one are you?

Polly Patience and Sally Scurry were not sisters, but they were really very alike to look at. It was only when you looked into their eyes, and listened to their voices, and watched them for a few moments that you

could tell which was which.

Polly Patience had deep, steady eyes, but Sally Scurry's were always darting here, there and everywhere. Polly's voice was quiet and clear, but Sally's was up and down, quick and loud. Polly did things easily and smoothly, but Sally rushed here and there, knocked things over, and made a noise.

They were good friends and went about a lot together. It amused them when people found it hard to tell one little girl from the other.

One day Sally Scurry wanted to go and call on the Wise Woman, and ask her for a spell to make flowers grow well in the garden. Polly went up the hill with her and soon they came to the Wise Woman's little cottage.

The gate stuck, and Sally shook it hard to open it. She made such a noise. Then Polly slipped the latch, and the gate opened easily. They walked up the path.

Sally banged loudly on the knocker. 'I do hope she's in!' she said. 'It would be so silly to come all this way for nothing.'

Nobody came to the door, but it seemed to the girls as if someone was inside, for they heard a movement.

'She's in,' said Sally, impatiently. 'Why doesn't she come to the door?'

She banged hard on the knocker again, and made a dreadful noise.

'Don't,' said Polly. 'If the Wise Woman is in, she can hear you if you knock quietly—and if she isn't, what's the use of banging?'

'Oh, why doesn't she come?' said Sally, crossly. 'I shall go and peep in at the window to see if she's there.'

'No, don't,' said Polly. 'It isn't nice to do that. People don't like peepers. Wait here patiently.'

But that was just what Sally couldn't do. She gave one more loud knock on the door, and then went round to peep in the window.

The Wise Woman was there! She was bending over a blue pot on her fire, stirring and stirring, for she was making a spell! She looked up and saw Sally peeping in. She looked so cross that Sally scurried round to the front door again.

'She's there,' she said. 'She saw me. I expect she'll come now.'

Sure enough, the Wise Woman did come to the door. She flung it open and glared at the two little girls, who looked so much alike.

'How dare you peep when I am doing one of my spells?' she cried. 'How dare you shake my gate as you did? How dare you bang so hard at my door that you nearly broke it down, and made two of my jugs jump off the dresser and break! I was doing a spell, a most important spell which I couldn't stop for a moment.'

'We're very sorry,' said both little girls quite frightened.

'You are in such a hurry, you can't wait a moment!' said the Wise

Woman. 'I won't have such behaviour! I suppose it was Sally Scurry who did all the knocking and peeping. Which of you is Sally Scurry?'

Neither of the girls answered. Sally was too afraid, and Polly didn't want to say she was Polly, because then the Wise Woman would know the other was Sally, and would perhaps punish her.

'Which one are **you**?' said the Wise Woman, looking at Sally. Sally didn't answer. The Wise Woman looked at Polly. 'Well, which one are **you**? Have you no tongue? What did you come here for, if you can't speak a word?'

'We came to ask you for a Growing Spell for the flowers in our garden,' said Polly. 'You said that you would give one to any child who came this week. We both love

flowers, and we would so much like a spell to make them grow well.'

'Come inside,' said the Wise Woman. 'You'll have to earn the spell. Sit down at that table there. That's right. Now, here is a jigsaw puzzle for each of you. You must do it for me before you learn the spell.'

The Wise Woman put a box of tiny little wooden pieces in front of each child. Sally and Polly emptied them out on to the table. They were not surprised at having to do something like this, for the Wise Woman had many queer ways.

'Now I'm going to get on with my spell,' said the Wise Woman, going to her blue, bubbling pot. 'Don't disturb me.'

The two girls began to do their jigsaw puzzles. They were difficult. The pieces that fitted together were hard to find. It needed a good deal of patience to fit any together at all.

Polly went on with hers bit by bit, and wouldn't give up. She had plenty of patience, and worked steadily. But Sally grumbled, and

whispered, and turned the pieces over and over again impatiently, trying to find some that would fit.

'Begin at the straight edges,' whispered Polly. But Sally couldn't be bothered. She scattered her pieces over the table, she even slapped them when they wouldn't come right! She really was an impatient little girl!

She grew so angry at last that she threw all the pieces on the floor. 'I can't do it! I don't believe it can be done! You've given Polly an easier one than me!'

'They are exactly the same,' said the Wise Woman. 'See—Polly has done hers! Now you know the growing spell, Polly. Use it well!'

Polly looked down at her puzzle, which she had now quite finished. Written on it was the growing spell! She read it and learnt it by heart—but the Wise Woman would not let her tell it to Sally.

'No,' she said. 'A growing spell for flowers is not good for impatient children like Sally. She would use it too soon or too much, and the flowers would suffer. A growing spell must be used gently and patiently. And now, I know which one of you is which! **You** are Sally Scurry, who can't be bothered to do

the puzzle, and who banged on my door and peeped in at my window!'

Sally went red, and shook in her shoes. The Wise Woman turned to Polly. 'And you are Polly Patience, who went on slowly till you **did** the puzzle, and found the spell you wanted. Use it, my dear, and have a lovely garden this summer!'

'Thank you,' said Polly, and got up to go, still saying the spell under her breath.

'And as for you,' said the Wise Woman, turning to Sally, 'as for you, I think you'd better stay with me a bit and learn patience and manners and——'

But Sally wasn't there! She scurried down the hill as fast as she could go. Stay with the strict old Wise Woman? Not Sally!

Little Mr. Kindly

One day in the High Street of Little Village, an old woman stood at the kerb.

It was a cold winter's day. The wind blew right down the street, and everyone shivered. The smell

from the baker's was very pleasant to everyone, as they hurried by the shop, and past the old woman who stood nearby, selling a few shoe-laces.

Mrs. Grand came by, dressed up in her new warm coat. She hoped everyone would see it, for she had bought it the day before. She looked down her nose at the old woman by the kerb.

'Dirty old thing!' she thought. 'Her coat is all in rags.'

Mr. Rich came by, and stopped to talk to Mrs. Grand. He had a very big house, and a hundred horses. People liked to be asked to his house, and felt very proud if they could say they were friends with him.

'What a dirty, ragged old woman!' he said to Mrs. Grand. 'Really, these beggars shouldn't be allowed, should they? They make me feel quite uncomfortable.'

The two walked on together. Then along came Mrs. Hurry, on her way to a meeting. She saw the old woman too, and almost stopped.

'If I wasn't late already, I would stop and ask the poor thing to buy herself some hot buns at the baker's,' she thought. 'But I mustn't be late for my meeting.'

So she hurried on, and the old woman thought that she would never sell any laces that morning. Then two children came skipping by and they saw her.

They were going to spend some money at the toyshop. They laughed at the old woman when they saw her.

'Doesn't she look a funny old thing?' they said to one another. 'She must have found that bonnet in the dustbin!'

They ran off to spend their money. The old woman sighed. It was cold in the wind, but this was the place where most people came every morning.

Mr. Promise came along, and he stopped at once. 'Why, you do look cold!' he said. 'I'll tell you what I'll do—I'll send my servant along soon with a warm shawl. You'll like that.'

'Oh, thank you,' said the old woman, and Mr. Promise hurried along home, thinking what a kind fellow he was. But when he got home he forgot all about the shawl, so the old woman didn't get it after all.

One after another the people of Little Village came by. Mr. Mean wouldn't look at the old woman. Miss Dreamy didn't even notice her. It seemed as if no one would ever buy a single shoelace again.

Then Mr. Kindly came by. He was a cheery little man, with twinkling eyes and a red face. He saw the old woman at once.

'Why, you shouldn't be standing here all day in this cold wind!' he said. 'Haven't you a home?'

'No,' said the old woman. 'I want to get enough money to go to my grandchild over in the next town. She'll give me a place by her fireside—but I haven't sold a single shoe-lace this morning. And I'm so cold—and hungry—and tired.'

A tear ran down her cheek, and Mr. Kindly felt so sorry that he could hardly keep himself from getting out his hanky and wiping the tear away.

‘Now you come home with me,’ he said. ‘I’ve only got a bit of a cottage, for I’m a poor man. But you just come home and get warm and have a bite of something. Then we’ll see about getting you back to your grandchild.’

He gave his arm to the old woman and took her to his cottage. He put

his kettle on to boil, and made a cup of tea. He brought her some bread and butter with a dab of jam.

'All I've got, I'm afraid,' he said. 'But it's better than nothing, so eat it up. And look here—this was an old rug I once had. You can have it for a shawl. It's red, and it will look quite nice on you.'

'What's your name?' said the old woman, looking at him gratefully.

'Mr. Kindly,' he said. 'Not much of a name, you know—no Sir or Lord or Your Majesty about **me**—just Mr. Kindly.'

'I might have guessed that was your name,' said the old woman.

'Now you rest a bit, and when I get out my cart this afternoon to take potatoes round, I'll take you over to your grandchild in the next village,' said Mr. Kindly.

So that afternoon, when he got out his old cart, Mr. Kindly put the old lady into it, beside him, well wrapped up in the old red rug, and set off to the next village. All the people of Little Village saw him go.

'Look at that!' said Mrs. Grand. 'There's that Mr. Kindly with that dreadful old woman.'

'Who is she?' called Mr. Rich. 'Is she your mother, Mr. Kindly? You never told us about her.'

Mr. Kindly stopped. His twinkling eyes suddenly went stern.

'No,' he said. 'She's not my mother. She's not your mother either. But she's **somebody's** mother, isn't she? And why shouldn't I look after somebody else's mother? You're too grand to be a friend to an old lady, but I'm not. I'm just little Mr. Kindly, and I'm glad to be a friend to anyone!'

They then drove off smartly, and Mr. Kindly raised his hat and grinned.

'Rude fellow!' said Mr. Rich.

'Most impolite,' said Mrs. Grand.

'What manners!' said Mr. Promise, remembering the red shawl he had promised and forgotten all about.

'I don't understand people like that,' said Miss Dreamy.

'I hope **I** never have to call him friend!' said Mr. Mean.

Well—I don't know what **you** think—but I know I'd be proud to call Mr. Kindly **my** friend, wouldn't you?

House on fire

Robert and Kenneth were walking along the road one night when they saw a queer red light in the window of a house.

'Look!' said Kenneth, 'I believe that house is on fire! See that red glow! Quick—we'd better do something about it.'

'What shall we do?' said Robert, half afraid.

'You run to the fire station and tell the firemen,' said Kenneth. 'Go on! I'll try and get into the house and see what's the matter.'

Robert ran off. Kenneth went to the door of the house and rang the bell and knocked. Nobody came. It seemed as if the house was empty. The red glow was brighter now, and he thought he could see flames.

'I'll have to get into the house and see if I can keep the fire under control till the firemen come,' he thought. He found a little window open in the kitchen. He was small, so he easily slipped through.

There was a horrid smell of burning in the house. Kenneth didn't like it. He tore upstairs, and came to a room where flames crackled angrily.

'Here's the fire!' thought Kenneth. 'Goodness, it will spread to the whole house if something isn't done quickly. Oh, what can I do?'

He ran to the bathroom. There was a big pail there. He turned on both bath taps and filled the pail. Then he left the taps running to fill the bath so that he could run to and fro, and dip the pail in to fill it quickly.

He threw the water on the flames. They sizzled loudly. He ran back and got another pailful of water. The curtains of the room were flaming, and a small wooden table was burning too. The flames reached the wastepaper basket and that flared up as well.

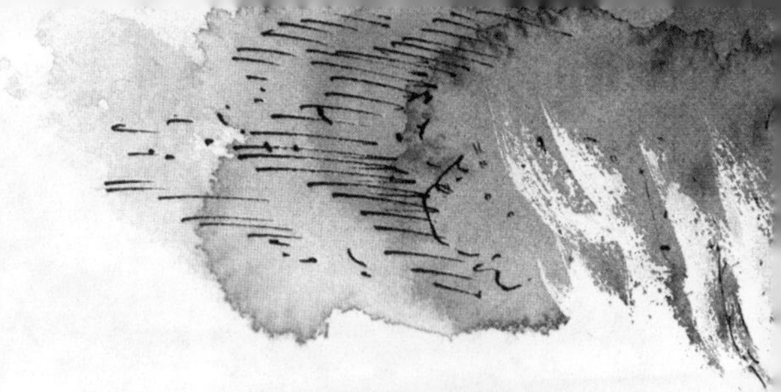

Then suddenly Kenneth saw something that made him gasp. In the corner of the room was a cot—and a small child lay there, asleep. 'Goodness!' thought Kenneth. 'Look at that baby! I must get it out of the room or it may be choked by the smoke or burnt in the flames.'

But the fire was between him and the cot. He threw pailful after pailful of water on the flames and at last made a pathway through. He rushed over to the cot, picked up the sleeping baby and ran back with it.

The flames leapt out at him as he passed, and burnt his eyebrows, and the smoke made his face as black as ink.

He ran downstairs and out into the garden. He didn't like to put the baby in any of the rooms downstairs, in case the whole house got on fire. He saw a shed, and put the baby there, still asleep, on a pile of sacks.

Then he ran back to the fire. He worked so hard! He dragged heavy pail after pail to the room, and emptied it on the flames. Sizzle, sizzle, sizzle!

The fire died down. It couldn't fiight against so much water. It was out! And just at that very moment up drove thc fire-engine, with Robert on the front of it, feeling very proud and important!

At the same time in rushed the owner of the house. She had been next door to fetch something and had stayed talking. When she saw the fire-engine she knew something had happened to her house, and she remembered her baby.

'Your house is on fire!' yelled Robert, who did not know that the fire was out. Then a man rushed up with a notebook. He belonged to a big newspaper, and he had heard about the fire. He wanted to know all about it so that the news could be put into the paper in the morning.

'I saw the fire!' said Robert, proudly. 'I fetched the fire-engine. I wasn't a bit afraid. If it hadn't been for me the whole house would have been burnt down, and everyone in it.'

'You're quite a hero!' said the newspaper man, and he took down Robert's name and address. 'Well done! We could do with more boys like you!'

Robert was very pleased. He talked to the crowd of people that had collected, and they told him what a brave and marvellous boy he was to see the fire and fetch the fire-engine.

'I say! There's no fire—it's been put out with water,' said a fireman.

'What's that you say, Madam—your baby is gone? Ah, here's a little boy who knows something about it, he says.'

It was Kenneth. 'Your baby's all right,' he said shyly to the weeping woman. 'I laid her safely in your shed when I put the fire out.'

The woman ran to get her baby. Kenneth didn't want to stay any longer, and he went home. He didn't say a word to anyone. He had done what he could, and thank goodness he had saved the baby and put out the fire. It was too bad that the fire-engine had turned out for nothing—still, it might have been useful if he hadn't been able to put out the fire himself.

'Look here,' said the newspaper man to Robert, 'look here, son, it seems to me there must have been another boy with you. The one who put the baby in the shed. Who was he? He seems to have gone home.'

'Oh, that was Kenneth,' said Robert. 'He stayed behind to watch the house. It was **I** who fetched the engine. Goodness, it will be fun to see my name in the newspapers tomorrow!'

But his name wasn't in. Instead the story was all about Kenneth, the modest hero who had gone into the house, rescued the baby, and put the fire out all by himself!

'This boy was so modest that he went home afterwards without saying anything about what he had done. He did not boast as another boy might have done. He did not even tell his mother, but went and had a bath and tried to clean up his clothes,' said the story in the paper. 'We take our hats off to little Kenneth!'

Robert tried to boast to the other boys about how he had fetched the fire-engine and ridden on the front. But nobody listened to him. They crowded round Kenneth and clapped him on the back and said how proud they were of him.

As for his mother she could hardly believe her eyes when she saw the story in the papers. 'Oh Kenneth!' she said, 'you **are** a brave little fellow—and to think you never said a word. Why, Robert said more about fetching the fire-engine than you said about putting out the fire and saving the baby. I'm proud of you!'

Well, of course, we do like to make our mothers proud of us—and you may be sure that pleased Kenneth more than anything else.